BY GARY WITTNER

*This book is dedicated with love to the
memory of my father, Robert D. Wittner.*

Cover photo: Frank Driggs Collection

ISBN 978-0-7935-8753-7

HAL•LEONARD®
CORPORATION

7777 W. BLUEMOUND RD. P.O. BOX 13819 MILWAUKEE, WI 53213

Visit Hal Leonard Online at
www.halleonard.com

"...jazz is my adventure. I'm after new chords, new ways of syncopating, new figurations, new runs—how to use notes differently..."

—*Thelonious Monk*

THELONIOUS MONK
FOR GUITAR

CONTENTS

ACKNOWLEDGMENTS

I would like to thank the following individuals for their help and support:

Jerry Granelli, Greg Yasinitsky, Andy Jaffee, John Damian, Dave Liebman, and all the other great teachers I've studied with.

Steve Berger, Dave Demsey, John Hunter, Steve Johnson, Howard Johnson, Marguerite Juenemann, Paul Lichter, Tom McClung, Ken Parker, Dave Seiler, Michael Shea, Don Stratton, Bob Thompson, and all the other friends and musicians I've been fortunate to know for their support and confidence in me.

Clark Terry for being who and what he is for all of us.

Betsy Wittner, Russel Wittner, Mary Therese Duffy, and Evan Strom for their love and support.

Don Sickler for the original concept, and for many hours of notation lessons.

Mrs. Nellie Monk, T.S. Monk, and Gale Monk for their encouragement and friendship.

The immortal Thelonious Monk and his music, for being the most consistent thing in my life for the past twenty years.

PREFACE

Thelonious Monk—innovator, composer, pianist, improviser, and inspiration to generations of musicians. Much has been said of this musical giant, and anything I might add here would be redundant. Here is what some of the giants of jazz music have said about Monk:

"... I realized that Monk was my guru..."—Sonny Rollins

"He is truly the classic composer of jazz."—Chick Corea

"Monk encouraged me to emancipate the drums from their subservient role as timekeepers."
—Max Roach

"If I hadn't met Monk shortly after I came to New York around 1945, I wouldn't have advanced as quickly as some say I did. He showed me voicings and progressions. Charlie Parker would take me down to listen to Monk all the time and make me sit in with him."—Miles Davis

"Working with Monk brought me close to a musical architect of the highest order. I learned from him in every way. I would talk to Monk about musical problems, and he would sit at the piano and show me the answers by playing them."—John Coltrane

If anyone reading this has yet to experience the amazing world of Thelonious Monk's music, the above comments will hopefully serve to arouse your curiosity. The recordings are available (see discography), and the excellent documentary film "Straight No Chaser," available on video, is a great place to start.

This book came about through a series of circumstances that took place about thirteen years after my initial contact with Monk's music, which occurred when I was an amateur guitarist and a pre-veterinary student at Cornell University. It was there that I first heard a Thelonious Monk record... it was love at first sound. Immediately hooked, I left Cornell and enrolled at Berklee College of Music, where I started transcribing, studying, and performing Monk's music.

In 1982, I began presenting all-Monk concerts and lecturing on his life and music throughout the United States and Europe. Over a decade later, I met T.S. Monk, Thelonious's son (and a wonderful musician in his own right), and asked if I could check my transcriptions with the originals. He put me in touch with Don Sickler, a vast source of information regarding this music. It was Don who, upon learning that I was a guitarist, not a pianist, had the idea for this book of Monk's music transcribed for the guitar.

INTRODUCTION

Each transcription in this book is accompanied by a set of performance notes. The notes are intended to supplement the notation with suggested fingerings, harmonic analysis, alternative voicings, and clarification of the song form. At the beginning of each set of notes is a list of the recordings used for the transcription. The arrangements utilize different parts of each recording because specific sections translated more easily than others from the piano to the guitar. Also, Monk varied the rhythms, voicings, and harmonies in specific places on each recording. When these differences occurred, I chose the rhythms and voicings that were most common, or I used one rhythm in the first A section and a variation in the second or last A section. These issues are referred to in the appropriate measures of the performance notes.

It should also be mentioned here that the guitar, though capable of many possibilities, was at an inherent disadvantage in this project. Monk had a maximum of ten fingers available (not to mention the occasional elbow), while the guitar is limited to six strings. In addition, the use of chords with seconds is a large part of Monk's harmonic vocabulary, and these are not nearly as playable on the guitar. I did, however, include as many of these types of voicings as was practical. When faced with the issue of distilling a larger voicing down to guitar size, I again consulted the recordings and chose those notes I felt gave the voicing the most authentic sound.

I have no doubt that the issue of playing such a distinctly pianistic style on the guitar will seem futile to some. In response, my own personal experience has shown this pursuit to be vastly rewarding in several ways. Not only has it led me to approach my instrument in a somewhat "un-guitarish" manner, but it has also been a fantastic musical education. My study of Monk's music is a continuing lesson in improvisation, compositional construction, harmony, rhythm, and creativity.

The transcriptions in this book are not simple, but do not be discouraged by this. Take your time, listen to the originals as much as possible, and practice everything slowly at first. They become easier as you listen to the recordings and get used to some of the techniques. Remember, too, that these compositions are vehicles for improvisation; once you start getting comfortable with the piece as written, there is another world of improvisation to explore. I say this not with the intention to intimidate, but to remind you of how many interesting and exciting possibilities lie within these pages. I'm still discovering new ones myself! Have fun!!!

AUTHOR'S NOTE

The music in this book is notated in the following manner:

1. Roman numerals are position markers. They indicate location of the first finger or, in some cases, the lowest note.

2. Left hand fingerings that do not fall within the position are indicated by numbers placed near the notes, usually to the left:

    1 = index finger, 2 = middle finger, 3 = ring finger, 4 = pinky

3. String numbers are used infrequently because they can be inferred by position and fingering.

SELECTED DISCOGRAPHY ON CD

Blue Note Records

Thelonious Monk: The Complete Blue Note Recordings, Blue Note 30363

Prestige, Riverside, and Milestone Records

Thelonious Monk Trio, OJC-001

Monk, OJC-016

Thelonious Monk Plays Duke Ellington, OJC-024

Brilliant Corners, OJC-026

Thelonious Monk with John Coltrane, OJC-039

Thelonious Monk and Sonny Rollins, OJC-059

The Unique Thelonious Monk, OJC-064

Monk's Music, OJC-084

Thelonious In Action, OJC-103

The Thelonious Monk Orchestra at Town Hall, OJC-135

Misterioso, OJC-206

Alone in San Francisco, OJC-231

Thelonious Himself, OJC-254

At the Blackhawk, OJC-305

5 by Monk by 5, OJC-362

Monk In Italy, OJC-488

Monk In France, OJC-670

San Francisco Holiday, M-9199

Thelonious Monk and the Jazz Giants, Riverside 60-118

The Complete Riverside Recordings, Riverside RCD-022

Columbia Records

Monk's Dream, CK-40786

Criss Cross, CK-48823

Straight, No Chaser, CK-64886

Underground, CK-40785

Monk's Blues, CK-53581

Greatest Hits, CK-65422

Live At the It Club, C2K-65288

Big Band and Quartet in Concert, C2K-57636

Monk Alone: The Complete Columbia Solo Studio Recordings of Thelonious Monk (1962-1968), Columbia/Legacy C2K-65495

Miscellaneous

The Complete London Recordings, Black Lion 7601

RUBY, MY DEAR
Performance Notes

Sources:

Genius of Modern Music, Blue Note 30363

Monk's Music, OJC-084

Thelonious Monk with John Coltane, OJC-039

Thelonious Alone in San Francisco, OJC-231

Solo Monk, C2K-65495

The Man I Love, Black Lion 7601

"Ruby, My Dear" was recorded seven times between 1947 and 1971. Originally, it had an alternate title, "Manhattan Moods." The melody is thirty-two measures long, in standard AABA form. Several of the recordings, however, follow an interesting AABABA form, where Monk goes back to the bridge after stating the full melody.

Measure 4: The Fm7 chord on beat 1 should be held while the G melody note is played on beat 2. Notice that the G is also held, and sustains as the top voice of the B♭13♭9 chord on beat 3. This is a difficult stretch, but it can be attained with practice. The alternate fingering moves this passage to the first position, where the Fm7 and B♭13♭9 chords can be played with a barre at the first fret. The B♮, notated as C♭ (♭9 of the B♭13♭9 chord), is played on the open second string.

Measure 5: The B♭ melody is in the middle of the E♭maj7 chord on beat 1. It should sustain for one and a half beats. The remaining chord tones should be muted by quickly lifting off the left hand fingers. The alternate harmony for beat 1 voices the B♭ melody on top, supported by a minor second (D-E♭). Beats 3 and 4 use passing chords to approach the Gm7 chord in measure 6. The alternate reharmonization for beat 4 uses a maj7 substitution for the A♭6 chord. Measure 13 is another variation on this phrase.

Measure 6: Here the melody in measure 4 is moved up a whole step. Be sure to hold the Gm7 chord and the A melody note for their full time value.

Measure 8: Try playing the B♭m9 with a barre at the sixth fret, and the E♭7♭9 with a barre at the fifth fret.

Measure 10: Notice the chromatic bass line moving from B♭ to A. The alternate reharmonization uses bass motion of a flatted fifth (E♭-A) by substituting an E♭7sus4 for the B♭m11. The second alternate moves the Amaj6/9 to second position.

Measure 11: The alternate harmony substitutes Bm11 for the E7sus4 on beat 1. The voicings are similar, however, the reharmonization creates strong chromatic bass motion to the B♭+7. Note the B♭+7 is voiced with the ♭7 and the root (A♭-B♭) on adjacent strings. This is a difficult stretch, but it can be played with practice.

Measures 12-13: Measure 12 is a ii–V progression leading to E♭maj9. Notice the octave displacement of the C♭ melody on beat 3, to C♭ an octave higher on beat 4. The melody resolves to the B♭ in the top voice of the E♭maj9 chord in measure 13.

Measure 14: This measure is a ii–V progression leading to Fmaj7. The Gm9/B♭ should be played with a first-finger barre at the fifth fret, allowing access to the G in the first chord and the A melody at beat 2. The alternate keeps the D♭ on beat 4 in the lower voice, resolving to the C in Fmaj7. Notice the C melody is harmonized with the minor second (E-F).

Measure 16: The melody line is C on beat 1, B♭ on beat 3, and F♭ on beat 4. Make sure to sustain the B♭m9 chord on beat 1 for its full duration. Lift the high F♭ on beat 3, allowing the melody to sustain.

Measure 18: The alternate harmony for this measure substitutes B♭m11 for E♭7sus4. Notice how this creates a chromatic bass line with smoother voice leading to the Amaj6/9.

Measures 22-23: Be sure to sustain the melody while playing the sixteenth-note bass line. The indicated fingering in fifth position requires a reach to the F♯, making it difficult to sustain the melody. Try the alternate fingering in second position: it allows you to play the E♮ and the F♯ on the fourth string, and the A bass note on the open fifth string. Beats 3 and 4 of measure 23 are Monk's fills, and were played differently on various recordings.

Measure 24: Try playing the Cm7 with a first finger barre at the eighth fret. This enables you to sustain the chord for its full time value, and allows you to stay in position to play the melody on beat 2.

Measure 25: The alternate voicing for the Cm7 chord on beat 1 contains the major and minor 7th on adjacent strings. This is a difficult stretch, but it is an interesting chord with a strong resolution to the Dm7 chord on beat 3.

Measure 27: This measure is a transition back to the first melody statement. The alternate harmony adds the ♭9 (E♮) to the E♭7♯9 chord for stronger resolution to the Fm9 chord in measure 28.

Measures 34-35: On beat 1, try using B♭ in the bass of the E♭7sus4 chord, creating a B♭m11 chord. The E11 on beat 3 is an unusual voicing, with the 11th and 3rd on adjacent strings. You can also replace the G♯ with an F♯ a whole step lower. The F♯ can then be repeated as the next melody note. In measure 35, be sure to hold the A♭ for its full time value as you shift to the B7♭9 chord. Notice that this measure uses the same dominant ♭9 chord progression as the introduction. At the end of measure 35, return to measure 4 for improvisation over the form. After improvisation, the full melody is repeated followed by the coda.

Coda: Measures 36 and 37 of the coda are similar to measures 34 and 35. The remainder of the coda is played rubato.

Ruby, My Dear

By Thelonious Monk

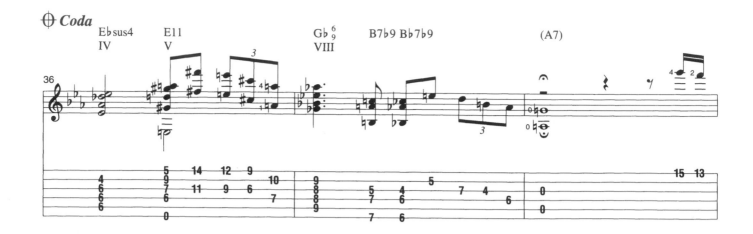

Coda

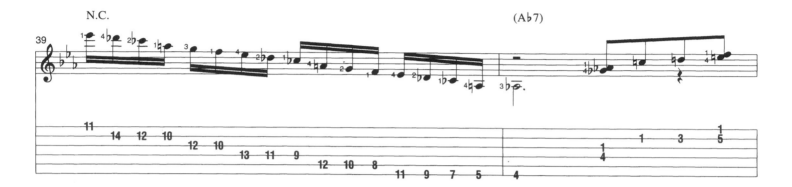

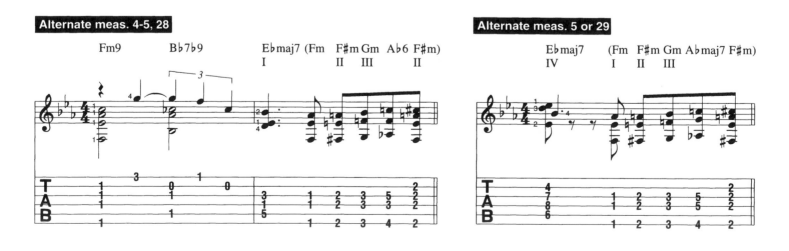

Alternate meas. 9, 33

Abmaj9   Cm7
IV

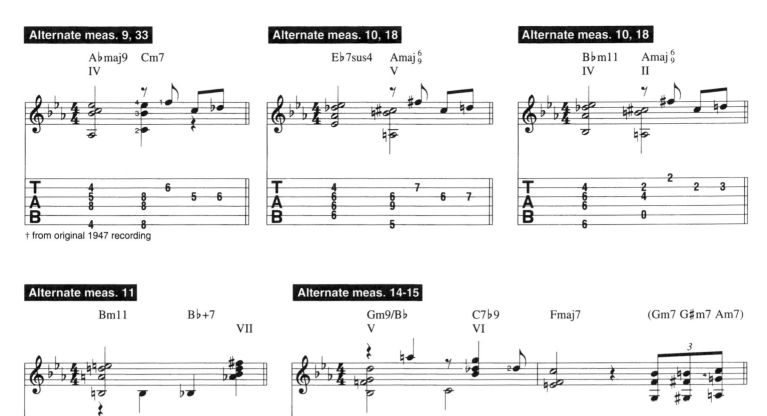

Alternate meas. 10, 18

Eb7sus4   Amaj$^6_9$
V

Alternate meas. 10, 18

Bbm11   Amaj$^6_9$
IV   II

† from original 1947 recording

Alternate meas. 11

Bm11   Bb+7
            VII

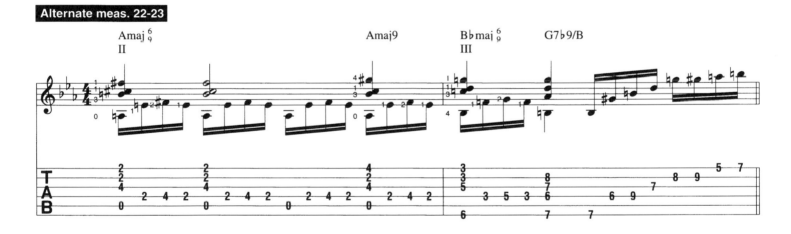

Alternate meas. 14-15

Gm9/Bb   C7b9   Fmaj7   (Gm7 G#m7 Am7)
V   VI

Alternate meas. 22-23

Amaj$^6_9$ Amaj9   Bbmaj$^6_9$ G7b9/B
II   III

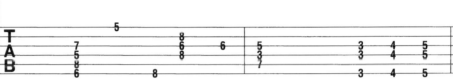

Alternate meas. 25

Cm7(maj7)   Dm7
             V

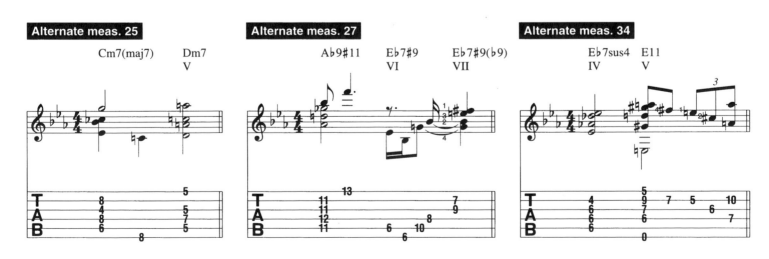

Alternate meas. 27

Ab9#11   Eb7#9   Eb7#9(b9)
          VI   VII

Alternate meas. 34

Eb7sus4   E11
IV   V

13

'ROUND MIDNIGHT
Performance Notes

Recorded Sources:

Genius of Modern Music, Blue Note 30363

Portrait of an Ermite, Swing 33342

Thelonious Himself, OJC-254

The Complete Riverside Recordings, RCD-022

At the Blackhawk, OJC-305

Live at the It Club, C2K 65288

"'Round Midnight" is probably Monk's most famous composition. It was originally recorded in 1944 by Cootie William's Orchestra, and then again in 1946 by Dizzy Gillespie. Monk recorded the song nine times between 1947 and 1968. The introduction included here was actually written by Dizzy Gillespie, and was used in Monk's original recording of the song. The Latin tag often associated with the song, also written by Gillespie, was not used in Monk's original recording. It is not included in this arrangement; however, Monk did use it in some later recordings.

Measure 1: Try playing the first half-note chord with a barre at the fifth fret. This allows access to the melody in fifth position on beats 1 and 2. As an alternative, you can play a similar half-note chord on the open third and fifth strings, and move the melody to the B and E strings. The primary melody on beat 4 is the D on top of the major second.

Measure 3: The fingering for this passage is the same as measure 1, moved down a whole step. Notice that the major second on beat 4 is omitted.

Measure 4: Use your first finger to play the E and C bass notes. Be sure to hold the C when playing the sixteenth notes on beat 2.

Measure 6: Beats 2 and 3 are augmented triads. Try playing them with downstrokes for better phrasing.

Measure 7: The diminished triads on beats 3 and 4 are played on the top three strings and moved up the neck by intervals of a minor third. You may want to experiment with playing the diminished triads on the B, G, and D strings, and combining them with the indicated fingerings.

Measure 8: The triplet figure starting with the E on beat 3 is a rhythm that Monk used quite often. Notice that it uses all the notes of a B♭ whole tone scale.

Measure 10: You may find it helpful to barre the fourth fret when playing the triplet figure on beat 2. This fingering allows easy access to the A♭ bass note on beat 3. Be sure to sustain the melody and bass note on beat 3 for their full duration. The high D♭ on beat 4 is an eighth note and should be lifted off, allowing the A♭ melody to sound.

Measure 11: The E♭ bass on beat 2 is an eighth note, with the ascending thirds played on the first and second strings. It is possible to play this measure with a barre at the eleventh fret, playing the thirds in position on adjacent strings. This is a difficult alternative; however, it does create more sustain in the bass.

Measure 12: Notice that the chords move in fourths while creating a chromatic bass line resolving to A♭m7 in measure 13. The alternate harmony for this measure doubles the melody in the middle voice. A variation of this phrase reoccurs in measure 20.

Measure 14: On beat 3, play the entire A♭7♭5 voicing, then lift off all of the notes except the D melody. Be sure that no open strings sound in the process. The lift can be quicker than the indicated eighth note if necessary. This technique of playing a chord, and suddenly removing all the notes except one, was a favorite of Monk's. It is used again on beat 1 of measure 16.

Measure 20: The melody line A–G♯–A♭–G♮ is in the middle voice of the chords. Measures 4 and 12 and their alternates are similar to this measure.

Measure 22: The triplet on beat 2 can be played several different ways. The main idea is to get the second finger on the D♭ for a smooth transition to the A♭7♭5 chord on beat 3. This phrase is similar to measure 14 and its alternate harmony.

Measure 23: The chord progression in this measure resolves to the E♭6 chord at the end the composition. Note the rhythmic variation of the melody in the first alternate, where the resolution to E♭ occurs in the final measure.

Measures 26 and 28: The melody is the higher voice in each of the seconds. Make sure those notes sound clearly.

Measure 27: The triplet on beat 1 is an embellishment of the melody.

Measure 29: The third-finger stretch on the triplet at beat 2 is difficult at first but attainable with practice. You can also use the fourth finger, but then sustaining the high C♭ becomes problematic. Be sure to hold the high B♭ for beats 3 and 4. This phrase is repeated in measure 32. Notice that the alternate harmony shifts the B♭ melody to the second half of beat 3.

Measure 30: The melody is the G♭ of beats 1 and 2, and the F on beats 3 and 4. The rest of the measure is Monk's embellishment.

'Round Midnight

Words by Bernie Hanighen
Music by Thelonious Monk and Cootie Williams

Intro

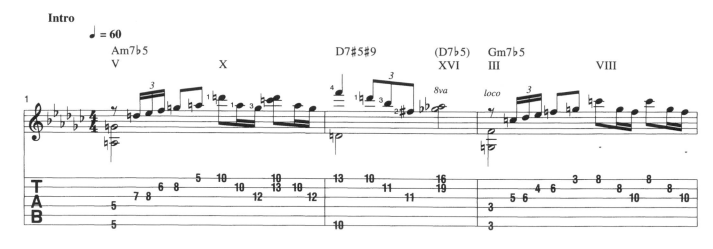

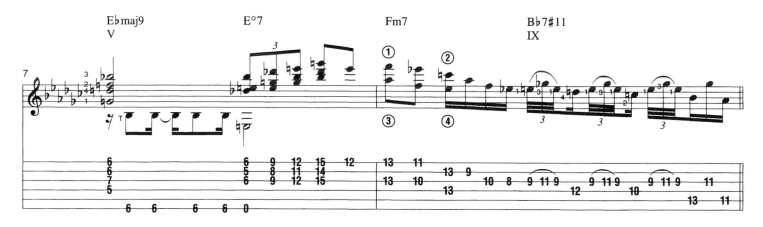

A **Melody**

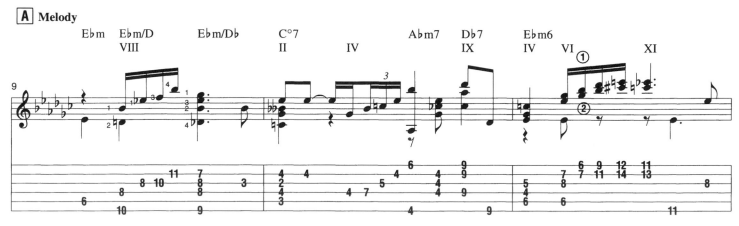

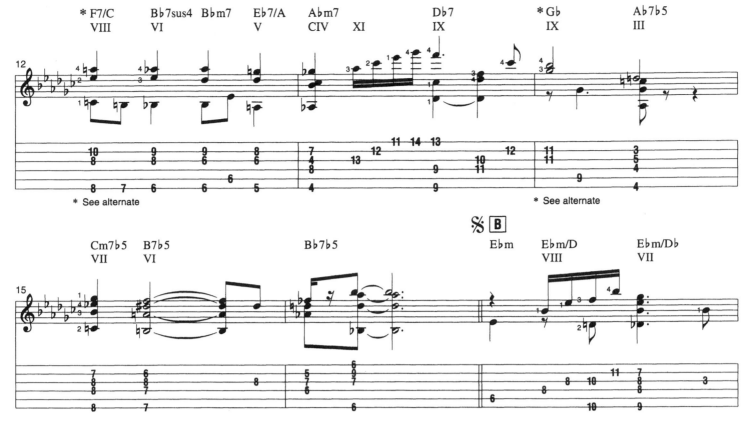

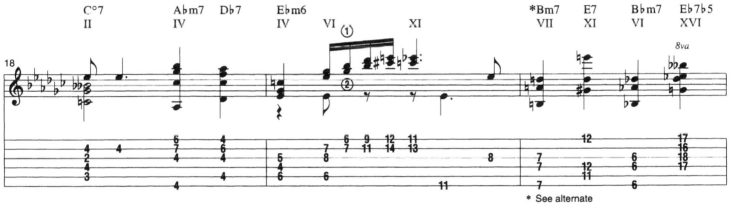

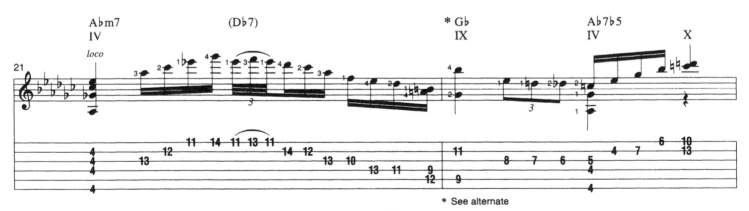

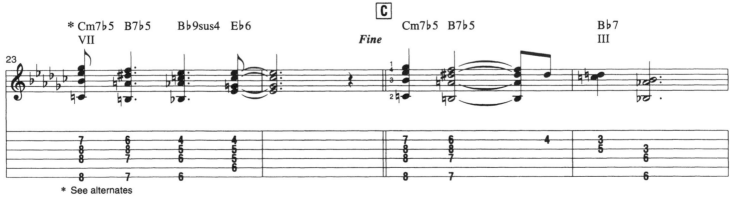

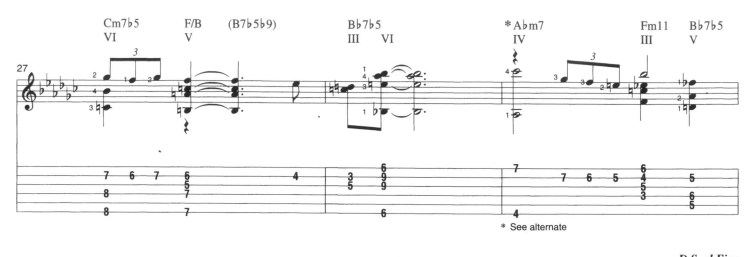

* See alternate

D.S. al Fine

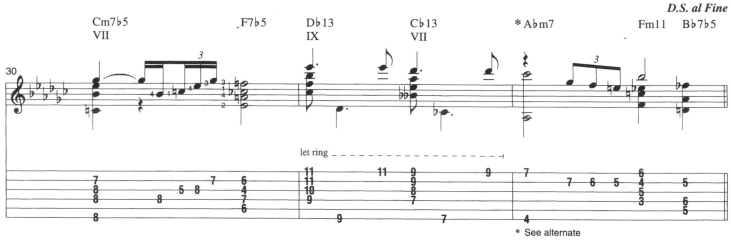

* See alternate

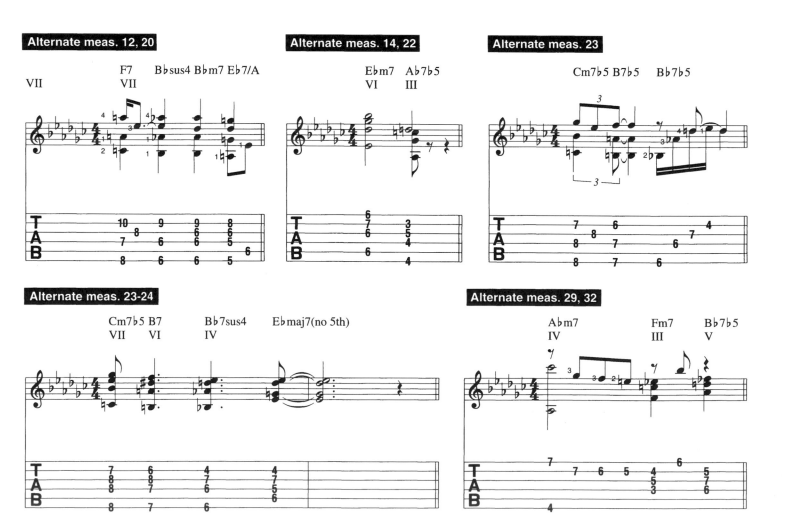

LITTLE ROOTIE TOOTIE
Performance Notes

Recorded Sources:

Monk, OJC-016

The Thelonious Monk Orchestra at Town Hall, OJC-135

Monk's Blues, Columbia CK-53581

The Complete London Recordings, Black Lion 7601

Many of Monk's compositions were reflections of his life and family. This piece was named after "Toot," the nickname for Monk's son. It was recorded in 1952, 1958, and 1968. "Little Rootie Tootie" is often referred to as Monk's "train song" because of the pickup chords, used prior to and within the second "A" section in measures 8 and 10. This arrangement is best suited for guitar and rhythm section. The melody on most recordings is played in unison with bass and horns.

Measures 1-2: Try using the fourth finger on the second string for the last triplet note of beat 2; this helps you make a smooth transition to the F on beat 3. The same type of common fingering is used throughout the piece each time this phrase is repeated. The second chord of measure 1 can be either dominant or minor—they were used interchangeably on Monk's recordings. The accompaniment for the last two beats of measure 2 was taken from the solo *Black Lion* version; the rhythm is similar to the sound of a stride piano. Be sure to hold the F from beat 2 while playing the E♭ bass note on beat 3.

Measures 3-4: The F melody note on beat 3 is harmonized with a major second (made up of the root and ♭7 of the F7 chord). Try to play this voicing with a downstroke, taking care that the E♭ does not mute the F. The alternate harmony for beat 4 of measure 4 adds the ♮9 (F) and ♯5 (B♮) to the E♭7 chord.

Measures 5-6: Make sure to play the C bass note in measure 5 on beat 3. This is the only significant difference between this measure and measure 1. Notice that the C functions as a leading tone into the D♭6 chord. In measure 6, play the D bass (on beat 4) with the second finger to make a smooth transition to the E♭ on the first beat of measure 7.

Measures 8 and 10: The triplet figure on beats 3 and 4 is not part of the melody, but it does occur with variations in most recordings of the piece. The piano voicing has an additional minor second (E-F) between the D♭ and the G. The entire voicing is impractical on the guitar, but you can experiment with combinations of these notes, taking care to keep the G♭ (notated as F♯) in the melody. Listening to Monk's recordings will also help.

Measures 9-12: The melody is the same as measures 1-4. The fingerings differ to facilitate movement to the triplet on beat 2. As in measure 1, use the fourth finger for the G♭–F melody line.

Measures 13-15: This section is identical to measures 5-7.

Measures 17-18: The melody on beat 4 of measure 17 is F–D♭. Be sure the melody can be heard clearly over the chords. Beats 2-4 of measure 18 are improvised; on some recordings, Monk plays the ascending thirds as tenths, moving the top note of the third up an octave.

Measures 19-20: Note how the last eighth note of measure 20 anticipates the F7 in measure 21.

Measures 21-22: The B♭ melody is voiced as the top note of the major second on beat 3. Try playing the preceding triplet with the third finger on B♮, the first or second finger on G♭ and high B, and then slide the first finger down one fret to play the B♭ melody. Now you can reach the A♭ on the second string with the fourth finger. In measure 22, note how the A♭ diminished triad functions as B♭7♭9. The alternate harmony shifts the melodic rhythm, and substitutes a Cm11 for the Fm7–B♭7♭9.

Measures 23-24: The melody starts with E♭ on the second half of beat 1 in measure 23, and ends with the high B♭ on beat three of measure 24. Note that the chord progression is a iii–VI–ii–V turnaround in the key of A major—a half step above the first section of the piece. The chords on the third and fourth beats of measure 24 move chromatically from E7 to E♭7, resolving back to the original key of A♭.

Coda: The coda is played only in the final chorus after the solos. Notice that the harmony is implied by the bass and the melody, rather than played as vertical chord structures. The solo chord changes are the same as in the 32-measure form, ending with measure 8. The bass notes of measures 27 through 30 of the coda can be doubled with bass, used for solo performance, or omitted.

Little Rootie Tootie

By Thelonious Monk

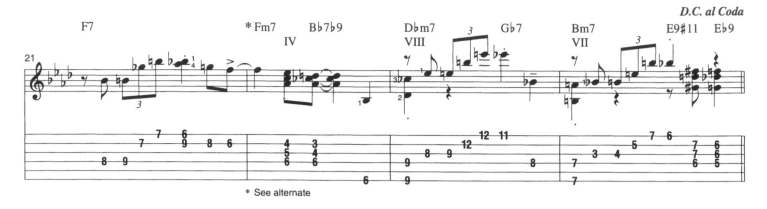

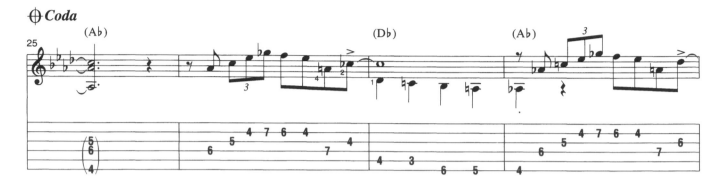

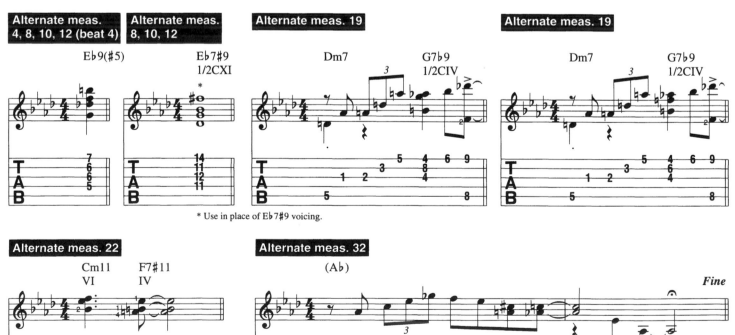

MONK'S DREAM
Performance Notes

Recorded Sources:

Monk, OJC-016

Monk's Dream, CK-40786

One of the many compositions bearing his name, "Monk's Dream" was recorded only twice: in 1952, and again in 1962, on the album bearing the same title. It contains an interesting use of harmonic rhythm in measures 7 and 15, where the phrase ends on beat 4 instead of beat 1 of the next measure.

This arrangement works well as a solo piece or with a rhythm section.

Measure 2: Try playing the Cmaj7 chord with the first finger on C, second finger on E, and the fourth finger on high B. Use the first finger to mute the open strings.

Measure 3: The F and B♭ on beat 2 are not part of the melody; this is a fill found on the recorded sources. The same phrase occurs in measure 5.

Measures 6-7: Notice that the alternate line changes the rhythm by shifting the accents to the second half of beat 4 in measure 6, and the second half of beat 1 in measure 7. The alternate can also be used for measures 14-15. All three variations are interchangeable and can be found in Monk's recordings. The original Prestige recording used the alternate version.

Measures 8-9: The D♭ on beat 4 is the final melody note of the first section. Try to hold the F in the bass for for the indicated duration. Notice the pickup notes on beat 3 and 4 of measure 9 lead back to the melody at measure 10.

Measure 11: The first two and a half beats of this measure are Monk's improvised fills. The melody resumes with the C on the second half of beat 3. The B♭ in the sixteenth-note triplet should be accented; try picking the first two notes of the triplet and pulling off from the B♭ to the second A♭. This figure appears again in measure 13.

Measure 18: Notice that the fourth finger plays the third string in each of the three chords in this measure. As you shift to play each voicing, keep the fourth finger lightly touching the third string, using it as a guide as you shift to the new chord. Be sure to keep a light touch to avoid string noise when shifting. This is a good technique for increasing left-hand efficiency when shifting positions.

Measures 22-25: The melody is the B♭ in the lower voice of the minor thirds. Note the alternate harmony of C7♭9/D♭. It is optional for improvisation.

Coda: When going into the solo section, the final G7♭5 (with the D♭ in the melody) is held across the bar line into the second measure of the coda. This is the final (32nd) measure of the AABA form used for soloing. The melody on beats 3 and 4 of the second measure, and the entire third measure, are played only at the very end (after solos) of the composition.

Monk's Dream

By Thelonious Monk

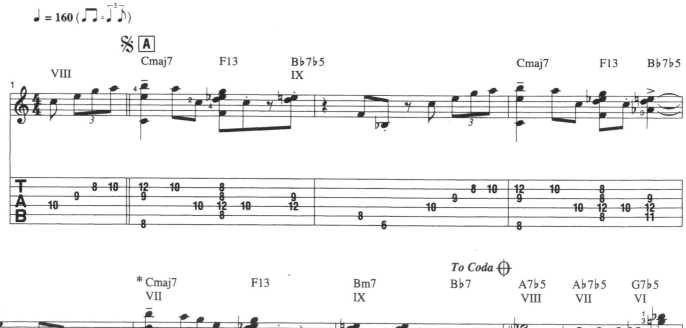

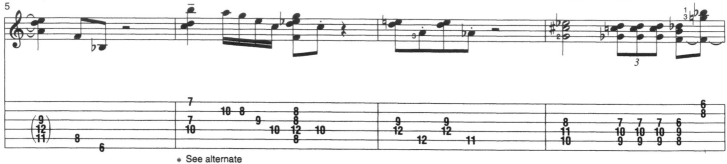

* See alternate

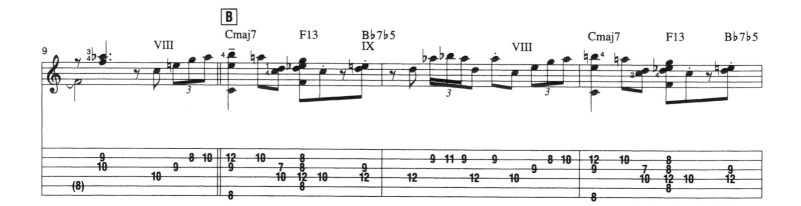

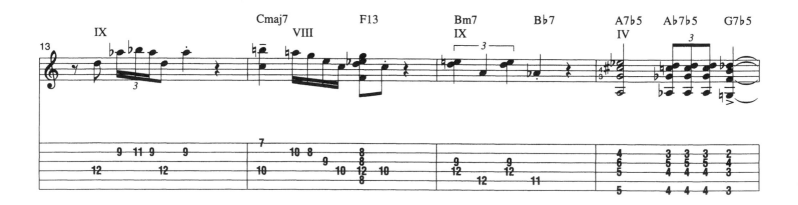

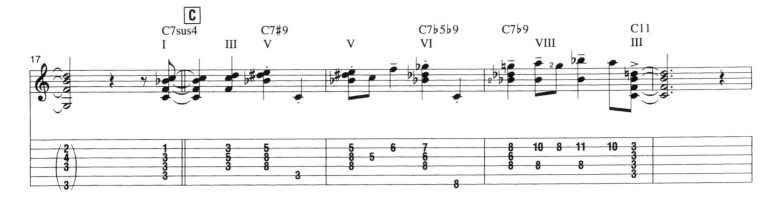

D.S. al Coda

* See alternate

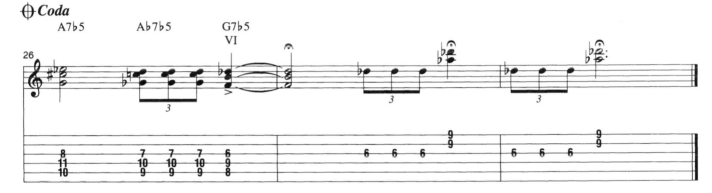

Alternate meas. 6-7

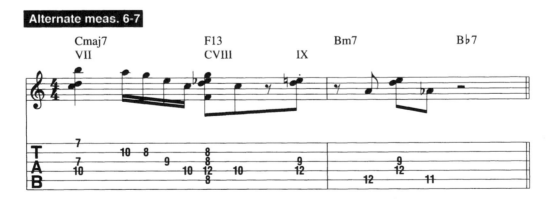

Alternate meas. 22-25

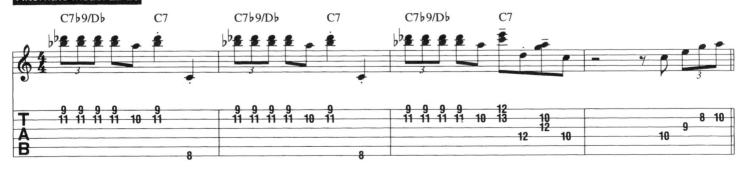

BEMSHA SWING
Performance Notes

Recorded Sources:

Monk, OJC-016

Brilliant Corners, OJC-026

Miles Davis All Stars, OJC-347

The Complete Riverside Recordings, RCD-022

"Bemsha Swing" was recorded six times between 1952 and 1964. It is a variant of the standard 32-measure AABA form. Each section is four measures in duration rather than the usual eight, making this a sixteen-measure AABA form. The composition is based on a four-measure phrase that is repeated in C, moved to F, and returned to C again. The harmony, in two-measure phrases, is an interesting study in turnarounds.

Measure 2: Make sure the C melody note is heard clearly; there is a tendency for the B to be louder than the C above it. If you are playing with pick and fingers, try the following right-hand fingering: sixth string, pick; third string, middle finger; second string, ring finger; first string, pinky. If you use a pick for the entire voicing, be sure to mute the D and A strings.

Measures 4-5: The D♯ on beat 1 is released almost immediately after it is played. Try picking the D♯ and the E with an upstroke to bring out the E melody. The chords on beat 4 of measure 4, and the first three beats of measure 5 are rhythmic fills played by Monk. The melody resumes on beat 4 with the major second F-G.

Measures 7-9: The melody from measure 3 is repeated and harmonized in thirds. This is a variation and does not occur on all recordings. The melody resumes in measure 9 with the C on beat 4. Notice how the chord progression shifts the key to F major for the middle section beginning at measure 10. Monk sometimes reharmonized the progression in measures 8-9 by substituting Cmaj7-A♭7-Gm7-C7 (or G♭7 for C7). Each chord receives two beats.

Measures 10-13: Note that the original melody statement in measures 1-4 is transposed up a fourth to F. In measure 11, try playing the G♭9♭5 chord with the fourth finger on the B string and the first finger on the first string. This allows you to easily reach the following B♭ melody note, and the major second G-A, in the fifth position at beat 1 of measure 12. The melody ends with the F in the A♭13 chord at measure 12. Measure 13 is Monk's improvised fill up to beat 4, where the major second F-G leads back to the final four-measure section of the melody.

Coda: The coda is played in each chorus. The A♭maj7 chord is completed by adding the A♭ bass note below the voicing on beat 1 of measure 15. You'll have to tap this note with the right hand if you hold the ties for their indicated durations. The A♭ bass note was not always played on Monk's recordings; sometimes the D♭maj7 was played two beats earlier than indicated in this arrangement. For solos, the indicated chords may be used; however, different recordings use variations of a I–vi–ii–V7 progression. Below are two alternate chord progressions that Monk used for the coda. Each chord receives two beats:

Cmaj7	–	D♭maj7	–	Cmaj7	–	G7
Cmaj7	–	B♭7	–	A♭7	–	G7

Bemsha Swing

By Thelonious Monk and Denzil Best

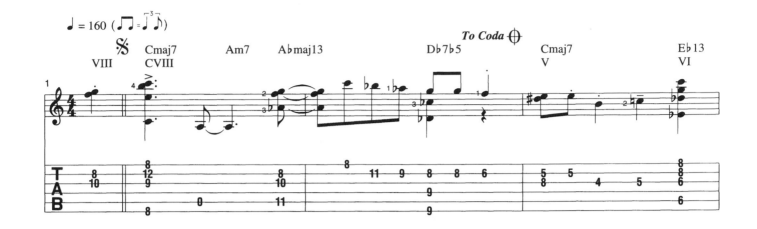

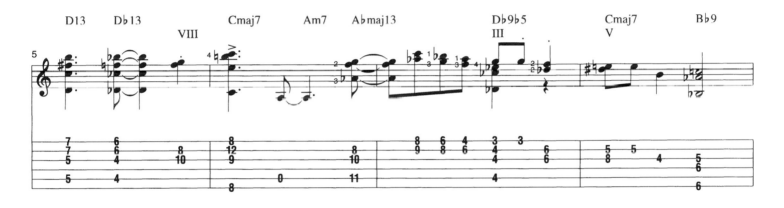

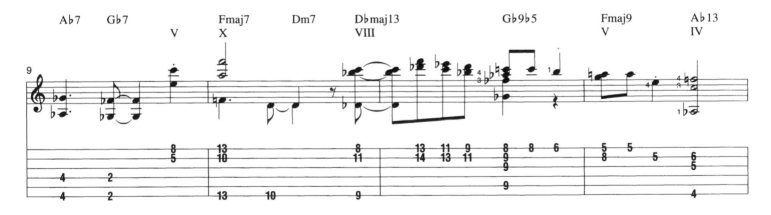

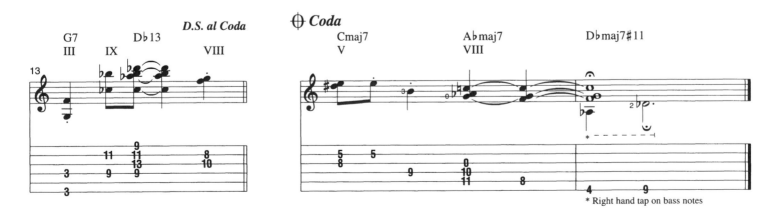

* Right hand tap on bass notes

REFLECTIONS
Performance Notes

Recorded Sources:

Monk, OJC-016

Alone in San Francisco, OJC-231

The Complete Black Lion and Vogue Recordings of Thelonious Monk, Mosaic MR4-112

"Reflections" was recorded five times between 1952 and 1968. The second recording, in 1954, listed the composition as "Portrait of an Ermite." It was originally a slow swing tune, but subsequent recordings treated it as a ballad, as it is most widely known today.

This is a solo guitar arrangement. There is quite a bit of activity in the bass line, and this works best unaccompanied.

Measure 1: Be sure to sustain the opening chord for the first full beat. On the end of beat 3, lift only the third finger to play the C melody. Let the rest of the chord sustain for the entire beat.

Measure 2: The E♭ bass line is Monk's addition to the melody. The rhythm used in this arrangement comes from one of Monk's recordings, but it can be varied according to your own taste. Try using an A bass note in the second half of this measure, creating an E♭7♭9 with a ♭5 in the bass.

Measure 3: Monk sometimes played the first three melody notes E♭–F–C as a quarter-note triplet. The second "A" section at measure 11 uses this rhythm. The melody line ends with the tied E♭ at the beginning of beat 3. The following sixteenth-note passage on beats 3 and 4 is Monk's improvised line. Note that the sixteenths on beat 3 are played *8va* (an octave higher than written). On beat 4, try to sustain the D♯ and the A until the B is played, to create a B7 chord (no 5th) on the final sixteenth note of the measure. For improvisation, the chord changes are A♭maj7 for two beats, B♭m7 for the third beat, and Bm7 for the fourth beat.

Measure 4: As in measures 11 and 12, the rhythm on beat 1 can also be played as quarter-note triplets.

Measure 5: On beats 2 and 3, the F is short, the C is sustained, and the D♭ is short. Be sure the C is still sounding after the D♭. This may be difficult at first; it may help to lean the fourth finger into the C after playing the D♭, almost as if invisibly playing the C again. The later recordings of this composition all used Gm7♭5 for this measure, and most players familiar with the song use this chord. The original Prestige recording, however, used a B♭m13. The chords are extremely similar with the main difference being the placement of the G. The bass movement, however, is much more interesting and unexpected with the Gm7♭5.

Measure 6: Notice the tritone substitution of E♭7♭9/A for the A7 on beat 3. It is common practice in jazz composition and improvisation to substitute a dominant chord raised an augmented fourth, in place of the original dominant chord.

Measures 7-8: The melody on beat 1 is the B♭ in the first chord. The C above it can be omitted or just played very lightly. Notice how the chromatic bass line in measure 8 creates a strong resolution back to the A♭maj7 chord in measure 9. Some of Monk's recordings use the chords in measure 8 for solos, while others simplify the changes to B♭m7-E♭7 for two beats each.

Measures 15-16: For solos, some recordings use slightly different chord changes: A♭maj7 (2 beats), B♭m7 (one beat), E♭7 (one beat); A♭maj7 (two beats), F7 (two beats).

Measure 19: The melody line is the triplet on beat 2, followed by the G on beat 3, and the final A♭ eighth note on the second half of beat 4.

Measure 20: The melody is the F whole note on beat 1. The remainder of the measure is Monk's improvised fill. You may want to experiment with the fill by using a different single-note line to imply the Fm(maj7) harmony.

Measure 21: The third beat is played with the B♭ melody held for a quarter note, punctuated with Monk's F minor chord played for only a sixteenth. Try to quickly lift the F minor chord, allowing the B♭ to sustain; be sure to stop the chord cleanly to prevent open strings from sounding.

Measure 22: Similar to measure 21, the melody on beats 3 and 4 should sustain while the voicing below is quickly lifted off. You can bring out the melody by playing the full chord with the melody note, then rapidly lifting all fingers except those playing the melody. Lift just far enough to stop the chord, and to prevent open strings from sounding. The same technique is used for the G in the second measure of the coda, and the D on beat 3 of measure 12.

Reflections

By Thelonious Monk

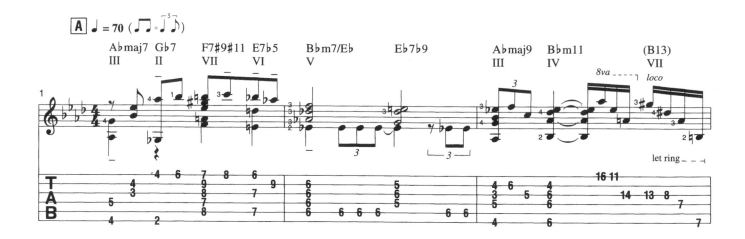

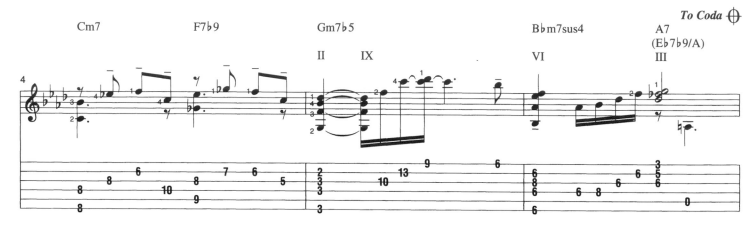

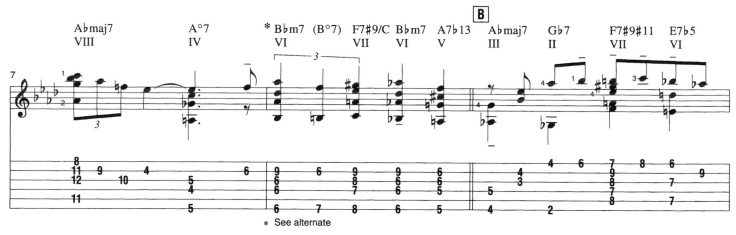

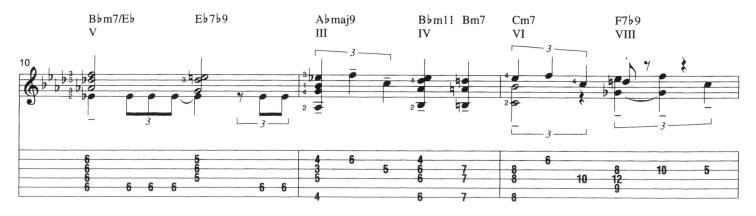

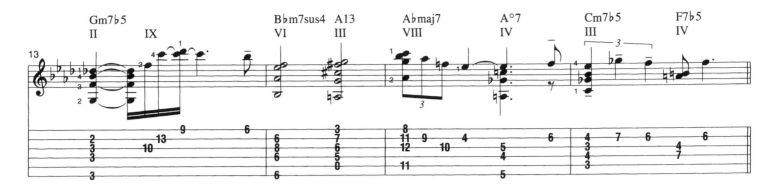

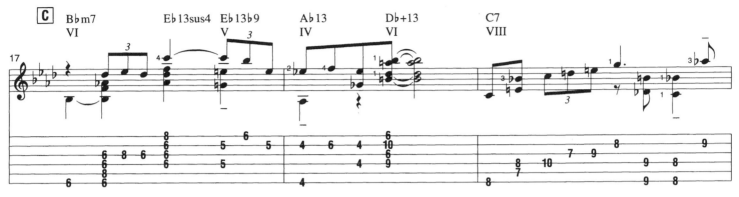

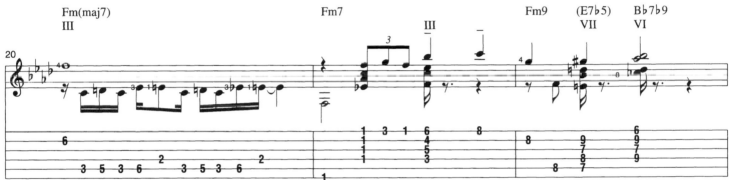

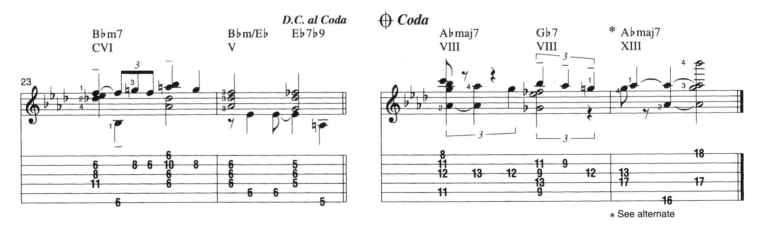

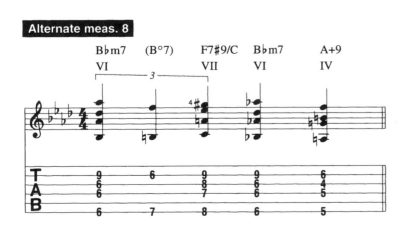

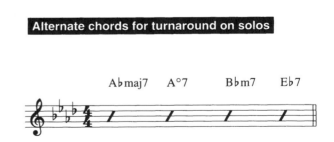

* See alternate

Alternate meas. 8

Alternate chords for turnaround on solos

WE SEE
Performance Notes

Recorded Sources:

Straight, No Chaser, CK-64886

The Complete Black Lion and Vogue Recordings of Thelonious Monk, Mosaic MR4-112

Thelonious Monk with Sonny Rollins and Frank Foster, OJC-016

"We See" was recorded three times in 1954 (the second was labelled as "Manganese") and once in 1966. The extended ii-V at letter C is reminiscent of other Monk compositions such as "Let's Call This," "Criss Cross," and "Hornin' In."

This arrangement can be played as a solo piece or with a rhythm section. The bass player should double the descending chromatic line in measures 1 and 9.

Measure 1: The opening melody note is D, in the B♭maj7 voicing. Note that it is voiced with a C♯ directly below it, creating an interval of a minor second. Be sure the melody can be heard clearly as there is a tendency for the C♯ to sound louder than the D. If you are having trouble bringing out the melody, try lifting the fourth finger from the C♯ just a moment before releasing the rest of the chord.

Measure 2: The melody notes (C and D) are voiced in seconds.

Measures 3, 5, and 11: The melody line is in the top voice of the parallel sixths. Since major and minor sixths are easy to play on the guitar, there may be a tendency to slide through these lines; try to articulate them as indicated in the notation. Note the alternate voicing on the second half of beat 4 in measure 3: it anticipates the F7♭9 with an unusual voicing of two minor seconds. You'll have to use your fourth finger on the fifth string to play the low A in this chord. It is possible to play this voicing in the third position, but it's a difficult stretch.

Measures 4, 8, and 12: These are Monk's improvised fills and can be played as written, varied by the individual, or omitted. They are useful when playing the arrangement as a solo piece, but less critical if playing with a rhythm section. Monk tends to use the fills more in the second "A" section (measures 9-16). Measures 20 and 24 also have Monk's improvised fills on the F7 chord. Try using the alternate whole tone phrase to embellish the F7 harmony in measures 4 or 8.

Measures 5-6 and 13-14: These lines are variations of the same melody. They are interchangeable phrases, and each can be used at either place in the form. The harmony is a ii–V leading to E♭maj7.

Measures 17-24: For improvisation, the ii-V in the bridge can also be Cm7/F, creating the sound of an Fsus9 chord.

Measures 18 and 22: The melody in these two measures is identical; notice, though, how the bottom note of each voicing alters the F7 harmony. Monk's first recording of this composition, on the Prestige label, used the E♭ and D♭ in both measures.

Coda: The chords in the coda are played in each chorus for solos.

We See

By Thelonious Monk

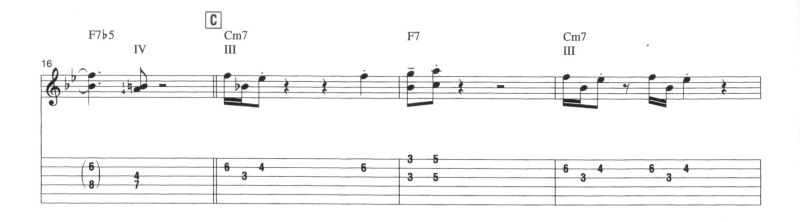

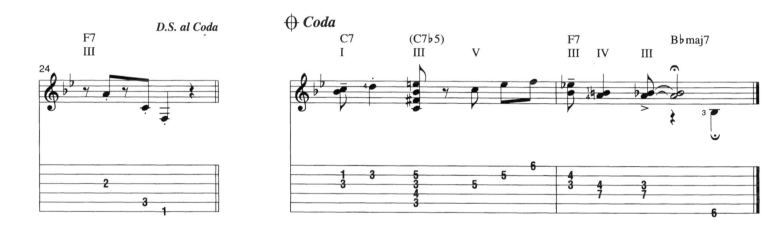

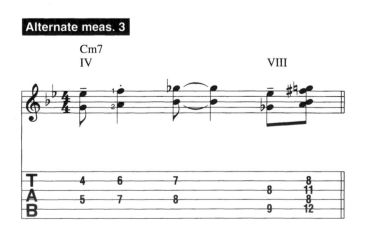

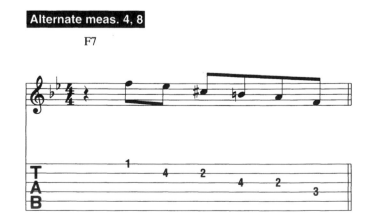

BLUE MONK
Performance Notes

Recorded Sources:

Thelonious Monk Trio, OJC-010

Art Blakey's Jazz Messengers with Thelonious Monk, Atlantic 1278 (LP)

Thelonious in Action, OJC-1013

Alone in San Francisco, OJC-231

Tokyo Concerts, Columbia 38610 (LP)

"Blue Monk" was recorded ten times between 1954 and 1965. It is one of his best known and most commonly played twelve-bar blues compositions. Like "Monk's Dream," the title uses the composer's name. A number of Monk's tunes have titles that refer to himself, family members, or places he frequented.

Measures 1-3: The B♭ bass in measure 1 can be played with the third finger, as the first and second fingers play the ascending thirds. The last third in the sequence (D-F) may be played with a full first-finger barre at the sixth fret, allowing easy access to the B♭ and A♭ on beat 4. For measure 2, you can use the same fingering, moved to the eighth position. As an alternative, the low B♭ on beat 1 can be played with the fourth finger; however, as the melody moves higher it may be difficult to sustain the B♭ for its full time value.

Measure 3: On beat 1, the high F and the B♭ bass can be played with a first-finger barre, as the second finger plays the D. The second third in the sequence, E♭-G, can be played by a barre with the third finger.

Measure 4: The notation suggests the A-C♯ major third be played with the second and third fingers, requiring you to release the B♭ bass and shift down to play the A♭-C♮. The alternate fingering uses the thumb to play the B♭ bass note; this approach allows more flexibility to play the melody and creates a smoother, more sustained, bass line.

Measure 6: The thirds can be played on the B and G strings using the second and third fingers for the first third, and the third and fourth fingers for the ascending thirds in the sequence. You may want to experiment with other fingering combinations that suit your own style.

Measure 7: Variations of this phrase recur throughout the piece. The low F in the triplet on beat 1 was not always played on Monk's recorded versions of this tune (see measure 4). When the F was used, it was held for varying time values, thus there are different fingerings for this phrase that are more or less interchangeable. Barre with the first finger to play the low F♮.

Measure 8: Hammer on the C♯ to D on beat 4. Notice the rhythmic variations of this phrase in measure 20, and in measure 8 of the alternate chorus; they are transcribed from various recordings of the song.

Measures 13-14: Note the added fifth and the flatted seventh of the B♭7 and E♭7 chords in each measure.

Measure 15: The fingering from the low E (notated as F♭) to the A-C♯ third is awkward, but it allows you to make a smooth transition to the B♭ triad with the bass on the sixth string. As an alternative, the A-C♯ third could be played with a barre on the second fret, and the B♭ triad played with the root on the 5th string. You may want to explore other fingerings for this passage that suit your individual style.

Measure 16: The A♭ on beat 2 is an eighth note and should be quickly muted while the other chord tones are held for their full time value. The A♭ can be muted by quickly lifting the third finger. Be careful to keep the string muted so there is no pull-off sound.

Measure 18: This phrase first appeared in measure 6. The last three notes are Monk's fills, not melody notes.

Measure 21: Everything after beat 1 is Monk's improvised fills.

Alternate chorus: This reharmonization of the main theme creates a different texture by voicing the melody in sixths. (This technique is repeated in measures 5-6.)

Blue Monk

By Thelonious Monk

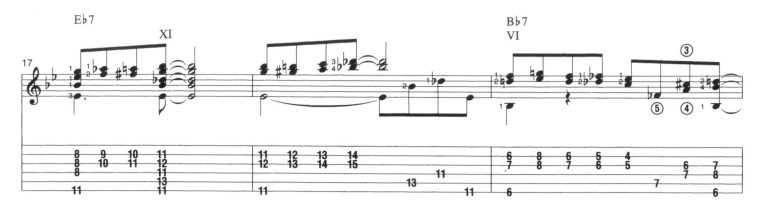

To Coda ⊕
†*Last time, D.S. al Coda*

⊕ *Coda*
* See alternate Coda

† repeat for solos

* See alternate Coda

Alternate chorus

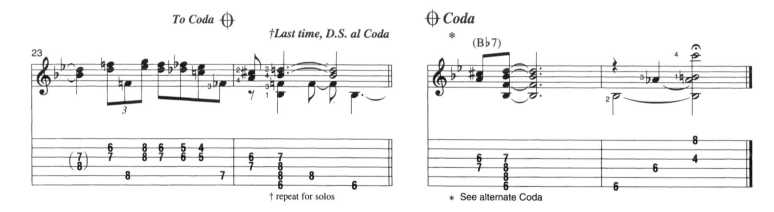

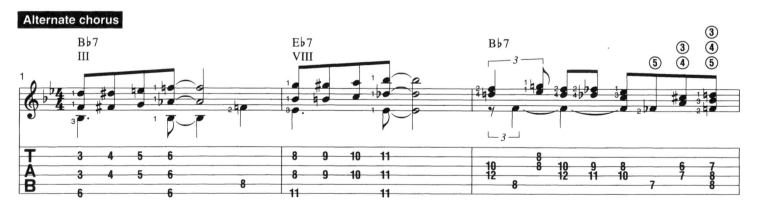

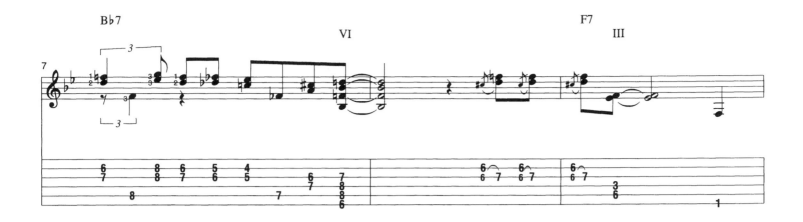

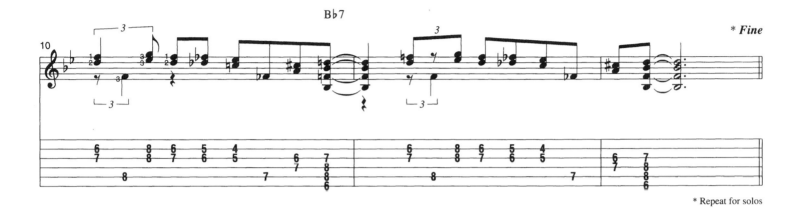

* Repeat for solos

Alternate meas. 4

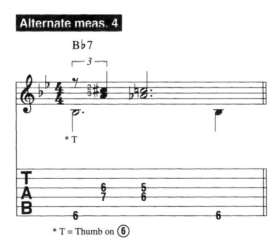

* T = Thumb on ⑥

Alternate Coda

NUTTY
Performance Notes

Recorded Sources:

Monk, OJC-016

Monk and Trane, OJC-039

The Complete Riverside Recordings, RCD-022

"Nutty" was recorded seven times between 1954 and 1971. Like "Bemsha Swing," it is based on a four-measure melody repeated in the tonic key (A section) and moved to the IV chord (B section). Here, however, the standard 32-measure AABA form is used. .

Measure 1: It may be a difficult stretch to hold the F melody note for two beats and also play the G bass note on beat 3. Try the following fingering: first-finger barre at the third fret to play the B♭, third finger on F, and the fourth finger on A. On beat 4, hold the barre with the fourth finger on A♭ and the second finger on B♮.

Measure 2: If you are using a pick, be careful to avoid striking any open strings as you move up the neck from beat 1 to beat 3. Try using the third finger on the E string for the A and F on beat 4.

Measures 3-4: This phrase looks harder than it really is. The chord on beat 4 of measure 3 is held, and the note F is played with the fourth finger. Sustain the outer voices of the chord, and play the C again on beat 1 of measure 4. The quarter-note triplet figure is not part of the melody, but it does occur in several of Monk's recordings.

Measure 5: Try using the fourth finger on the D string for the first two quarter notes of the quarter-note triplet.

Measure 8: This is Monk's improvised line using the F whole tone scale. Monk often improvised over this measure using the whole tone scale to imply an F7 augmented chord, creating a strong resolution back to the B♭maj7.

Measures 11-12: The voicing on beat 4 anticipates the F7 in the next measure using the 3rd, ♯9th, and 5th. The same voicing appears in the alternate to measures 19-20, raised a fourth to B♭7.

Measure 16: Similar to measure 8, this is an improvised passage played by Monk using the whole tone scale from B♭. The phrase implies a B♭+7 chord and creates a strong resolution to E♭maj7.

Note that the first five measures of the bridge utilize the first five measures of the tune moved up a perfect fourth.

Measures 19-20: Notice how beats 3 and 4 of measure 19 anticipate the harmony in measure 20. The voicing used on beat 4 of measure 11 can also be used here (raised a fourth), with the same resulting harmony of the 3rd, ♯9th, and 5th anticipating B♭7. This is notated in the alternate voicing for measure 19.

Measure 23: The melody note on the end of beat 3 is the C below the D. Try playing these two notes with a downstroke to make the the C more prominent. You can try to lift off the D a bit sooner to help bring out the C.

Measure 24: The melody is F in the major second on beats 1 and 2. The rest of the measure is Monk's improvisation implying the V7♭5 of B♭.

Coda: The last melody note in measure 27 is the D tied from the previous measure. The remaining material is an ending intended for the last time through the song. Note the last measure where the ♮9 and ♭9th are voiced a minor ninth apart.

Improvisation: The bass player often plays an ascending chromatic line from the root of the major seventh chord in the first two measures of each four-measure section (measures 1-2, 5-6, 9-10, 13-14, 17-18, and 21-22). This changes the chord progression from Imaj7–VI7–ii7–V7 (2 beats each) to Imaj7–♯i°7–ii7–♯II°7. The form for solos omits the last measure of the coda to retain the 32-measure form. A turnaround can be used in the second and third measures of the coda.

Nutty

By Thelonious Monk

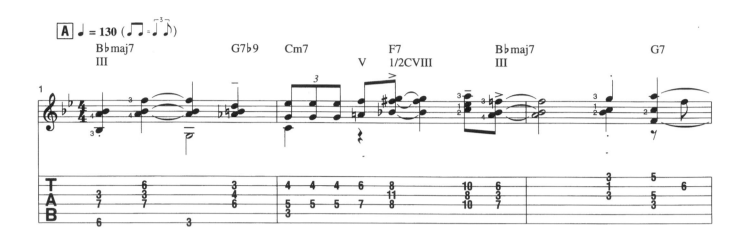

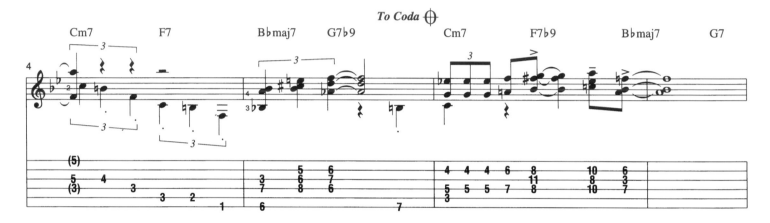

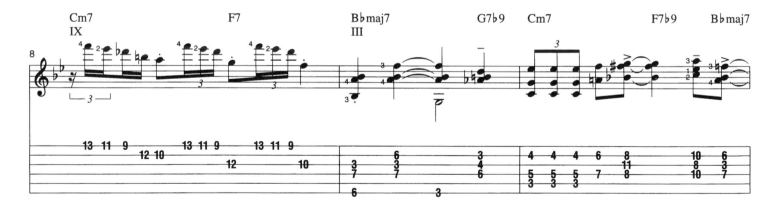

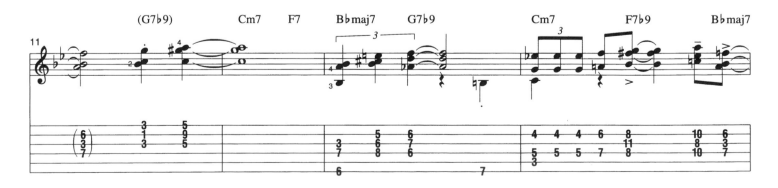

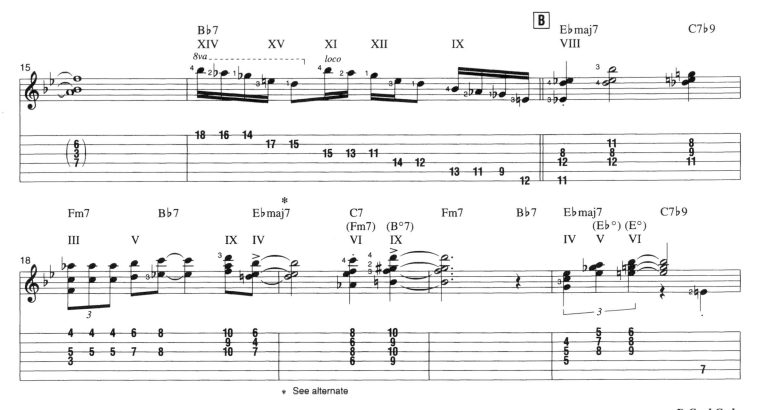

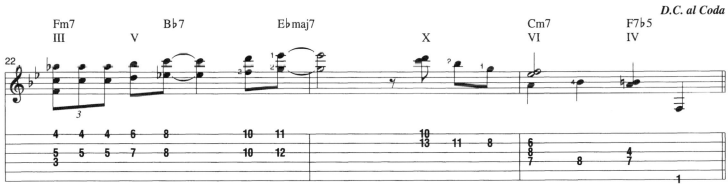

* See alternate

D.C. al Coda

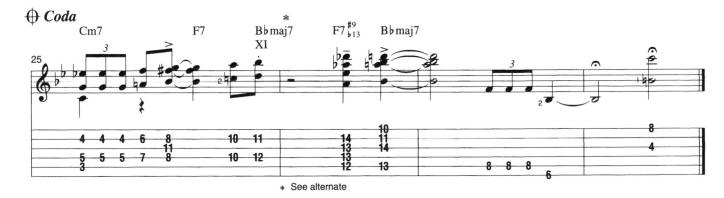

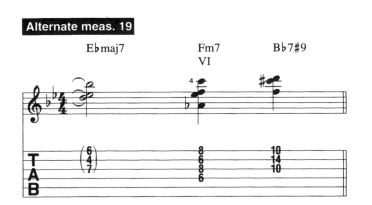

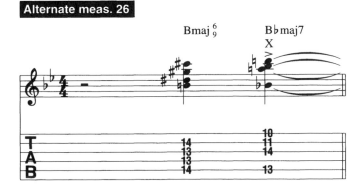

* See alternate

PLAYED TWICE
Performance Notes

Recorded Sources:

The Complete Riverside Recordings of Thelonious Monk, RCD-022

Live at Lincoln Center, Columbia C2K-57636

"Played Twice" was recorded in 1959 and 1963. It is a sixteen-measure tune with an interesting shift in meter and melodic rhythm. One recording starts the melody in measure 9 on beat 2, and then changes measure 12 to 2/4 time. The other version starts the same melody two beats later on the second half of beat 4, making measure 12 a full four beats.

This arrangement is best suited to be played with a rhythm section. Most of the activity is in the melody, with occasional chord voicings and minimal bass movement.

Measure 2: Monk occasionally used the same upper voicing on beat 4, as on beat 1. The indicated voicing on beat 4 adds rhythmic interest by anticipating the D♭13 chord in measure 3.

Measure 3: On the second half of beat 1, Monk uses a dominant seventh voicing with the 13 and ♭7 adjacent to each other. Note the four-note whole-tone melody from C♭ to F on beats 2 and 3. Use of the whole tone scale is quite common in Monk's music.

Measure 4: On beat 1, it is a difficult stretch to play the indicated fingering from the D♭ melody note to the D♭13 chord. Another option is to use your fourth finger on the C♭ on the second half of beat 1, and play the second half of measure 3 in eighth position.

Measure 8: The Gm7/C voicing on the second half of beat 1 can be played on beat 2 for rhythmic variation. The A melody note should still be played as written on the second half of beat 1.

Measure 11: As in measure 3, this is another example of how Monk used unexpected notes in dominant seventh chords. Notice that the 3rd and the 11th are included in the F11 voicing.

Measure 13: This measure is in 2/4 time when playing the melody, and 4/4 time during the solo section. Monk also recorded this composition with the melody in measure 9 beginning on the second half of beat 4, rather than on beat 2, as indicated here. The melody was still played the same way, resulting in the 2/4 measure becoming beats 3 and 4 of measure 13. The solos retain the same form, with four measures of F7 in measures 10-13.

Measure 15: Note alternate fingering for measures 3 and 7.

Measures 17-18: Make sure the melody (F♯ to D) is played clearly and not obscured by the lower notes of the chords.

Played Twice

By Thelonious Monk

* See alternate   * See alternate   * See alternate   * 4/4 for solos

Alternate meas. 9

Alternate meas. 11

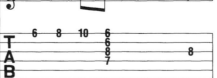

Alternate meas. 12

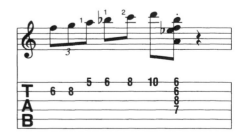

UGLY BEAUTY
Performance Notes

Recorded Source:

Underground Monk, Columbia CK-40785

"Ugly Beauty" was recorded once in 1967. It is the only waltz that Monk wrote.

The low E string is tuned down a whole step to D for this arrangement. This tuning allows you to play a Dm11(♭5/♯5) chord with the D-A on the fifth and sixth strings. This chord is the "Ugly Beauty" of the composition.

This arrangement works well as a solo piece or with a rhythm section. Be careful to avoid clashes with the bass. If performing this song live, don't forget to retune low D back to E before you start the next tune!

Introduction: The rhythm of the introduction is loosely interpreted with fermatas lasting for approximately two beats. All the notes, except for the D on beat 2 of each measure, are sustained as indicated. Strict time begins at measure 4.

Measure 5: The indicated left-hand fingering for G13♭9 enables you to reach the G bass on beat 2, while sustaining the rest of the chord for its full duration. Notice that the A♭ is played on the 4th string, and the G is played on the open third string. For an alternative fingering, play the E♮ with the third finger, G on the open string, and A♭ with the fourth finger.

Measure 8: The indicated fingering for the Em7/A♭ chord on beat 1 barres the sixth fret. Pick-style players will need to use other right hand fingers to play this voicing as written. Try using the pick on the sixth string, middle finger on the fifth, ring finger on the third, and pinky on the second. As an alternative, you could also use the pick and middle finger as indicated above, and then use the ring finger to play the second and third strings. If this is too difficult, you can strum through all five bottom strings, doubling the A♭ on the fourth string; however, the indicated voicing is preferable.

Measure 10: The melody is D♭ to E♭. Be sure to play the melody clearly while sustaining the D♭ and A♭ in the bass on beat 1. Notice that you can play the harmonized E♭ melody on beat 2 by holding the D♭maj7 chord, and sliding the first finger up two frets.

Measure 14: The indicated fingering places the high G on the second string. As an alternative, try playing the G on the first string while muting the B string with the first finger.

Measure 17: As notated, be sure to play the A-C minor third on the second sixteenth of the measure while holding the F.

Measure 18: This phrase is identical to measure 10.

Measure 19: The melody is the tied E♭ half note. The voicing on beat 3 is Monk's fill.

Measure 22: The B♭7♯9♭13 chord on beat 1 should be held as you play the bass note on beat 2. This is an awkward stretch, but it can be played with practice.

Measure 25: The stretch from the D7♭5 chord on beat 1 to the D bass on beat 2 makes it difficult to sustain the D7♭5 for its full time value. The A♭ on beat 1 can be played as a quarter note if necessary, but the indicated rhythms are preferable. The following fingering may be useful: barre with the first finger at the ninth fret to play the high A♭ and the F♯, then play the C with the second finger. This allows access to the low D with the fourth finger. Pick-style players will have to incorporate the middle and ring fingers of the right hand to play the C and the A♭. Be sure to avoid the E♮ on the third string.

Measures 30-31: Make sure the F melody note on the second half of beat 3 is held across the bar line for its full time value. Articulate the melody by playing the E-F minor second with an upstroke while holding the F with the first finger. Be sure to sustain the F as you play the D♭maj7. Use the pick to play the low A♭ and your middle or ring finger on the high C.

Measure 35: This voicing occurred previously in measure 10 and 18. The melody is the high D♭.

Ugly Beauty

By Thelonious Monk

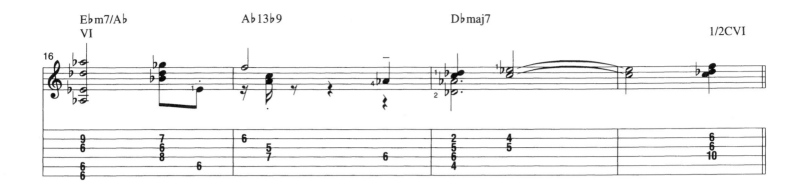

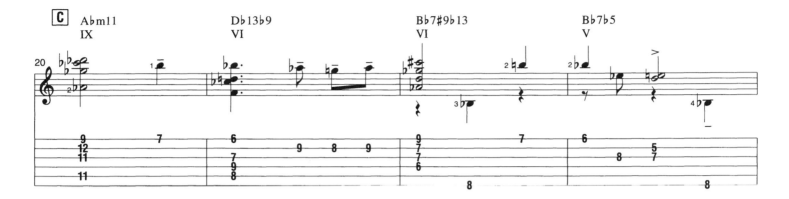

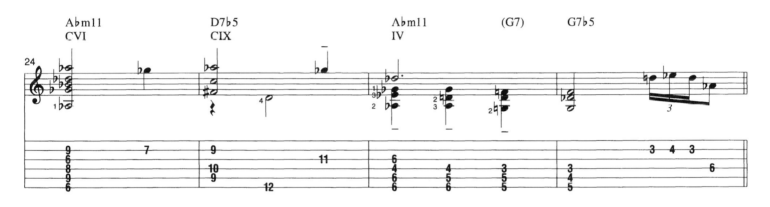

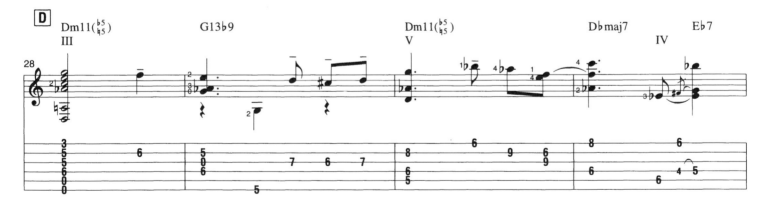

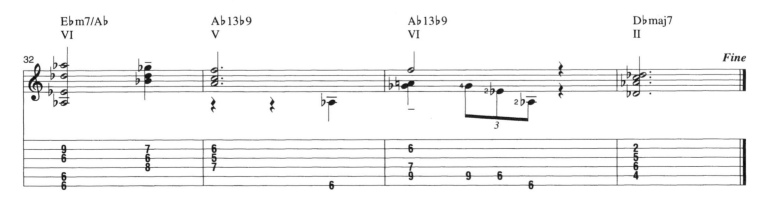

ABOUT THE AUTHOR

Guitarist, composer, and educator Gary Wittner began transcribing and studying Thelonious Monk's music in 1977. He graduated from the Berklee College of Music in 1981 and performed his first all Monk concert the following year. Gary completed his Master's Degree thesis, an extensive analysis of Monk's compositional style, in 1986. Since then, he has travelled extensively throughout the United States and Europe performing Monk's music and lecturing on Monk's music and life. He has been a featured performer playing Monk with Reggie Workman, Clark Terry, Eddie Gomez, Richard Davis, James Emery, Paul McCandless, and numerous others. Gary has also had several "Monk on Guitar" lessons published in *Guitar Player* magazine. A faculty member of the University of Maine at Augusta for eleven years (including one year as jazz department coordinator), Gary recently moved to the New York area to continue his work with Monk's music, and to focus his energies on his performance career. He is available for concerts and lectures and can be reached for more information at his e-mail address: gdwgtr@aol.com. There will also be a "Monk on Guitar" website describing Gary's work in more detail.

Guitar Notation Legend

Guitar Music can be notated three different ways: on a *musical staff*, in *tablature*, and in *rhythm slashes*.

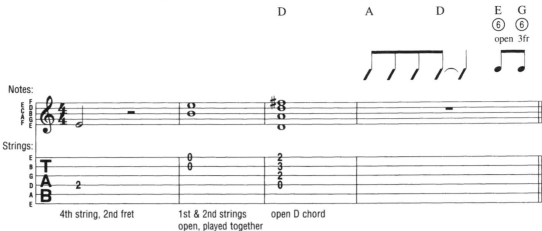

RHYTHM SLASHES are written above the staff. Strum chords in the rhythm indicated. Use the chord diagrams found at the top of the first page of the transcription for the appropriate chord voicings. Round noteheads indicate single notes.

THE MUSICAL STAFF shows pitches and rhythms and is divided by bar lines into measures. Pitches are named after the first seven letters of the alphabet.

TABLATURE graphically represents the guitar fingerboard. Each horizontal line represents a a string, and each number represents a fret.

4th string, 2nd fret

1st & 2nd strings open, played together

open D chord

Definitions for Special Guitar Notation

HALF-STEP BEND: Strike the note and bend up 1/2 step.

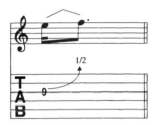

WHOLE-STEP BEND: Strike the note and bend up one step.

GRACE NOTE BEND: Strike the note and bend up as indicated. The first note does not take up any time.

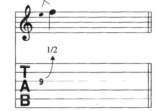

SLIGHT (MICROTONE) BEND: Strike the note and bend up 1/4 step.

BEND AND RELEASE: Strike the note and bend up as indicated, then release back to the original note. Only the first note is struck.

PRE-BEND: Bend the note as indicated, then strike it.

PRE-BEND AND RELEASE: Bend the note as indicated. Strike it and release the bend back to the original note.

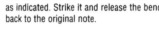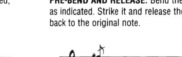

UNISON BEND: Strike the two notes simultaneously and bend the lower note up to the pitch of the higher.

VIBRATO: The string is vibrated by rapidly bending and releasing the note with the fretting hand.

WIDE VIBRATO: The pitch is varied to a greater degree by vibrating with the fretting hand.

HAMMER-ON: Strike the first (lower) note with one finger, then sound the higher note (on the same string) with another finger by fretting it without picking.

PULL-OFF: Place both fingers on the notes to be sounded. Strike the first note and without picking, pull the finger off to sound the second (lower) note.

LEGATO SLIDE: Strike the first note and then slide the same fret-hand finger up or down to the second note. The second note is not struck.

SHIFT SLIDE: Same as legato slide, except the second note is struck.

TRILL: Very rapidly alternate between the notes indicated by continuously hammering on and pulling off.

TAPPING: Hammer ("tap") the fret indicated with the pick-hand index or middle finger and pull off to the note fretted by the fret hand.

NATURAL HARMONIC: Strike the note while the fret-hand lightly touches the string directly over the fret indicated.

PINCH HARMONIC: The note is fretted normally and a harmonic is produced by adding the edge of the thumb or the tip of the index finger of the pick hand to the normal pick attack.

HARP HARMONIC: The note is fretted normally and a harmonic is produced by gently resting the pick hand's index finger directly above the indicated fret (in parentheses) while the pick hand's thumb or pick assists by plucking the appropriate string.

PICK SCRAPE: The edge of the pick is rubbed down (or up) the string, producing a scratchy sound.

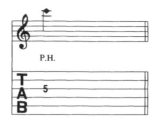

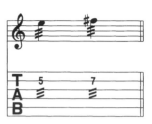

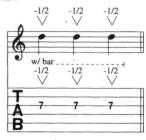

MUFFLED STRINGS: A percussive sound is produced by laying the fret hand across the string(s) without depressing, and striking them with the pick hand.

PALM MUTING: The note is partially muted by the pick hand lightly touching the string(s) just before the bridge.

RAKE: Drag the pick across the strings indicated with a single motion.

TREMOLO PICKING: The note is picked as rapidly and continuously as possible.

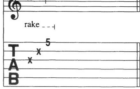

ARPEGGIATE: Play the notes of the chord indicated by quickly rolling them from bottom to top.

VIBRATO BAR DIVE AND RETURN: The pitch of the note or chord is dropped a specified number of steps (in rhythm) then returned to the original pitch.

VIBRATO BAR SCOOP: Depress the bar just before striking the note, then quickly release the bar.

VIBRATO BAR DIP: Strike the note and then immediately drop a specified number of steps, then release back to the original pitch.

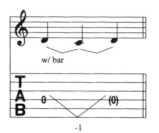

Additional Musical Definitions

(accent)	• Accentuate note (play it louder)	
(accent)	• Accentuate note with great intensity	
(staccato)	• Play the note short	
	• Downstroke	
V	• Upstroke	

D.S. al Coda — • Go back to the sign (𝄋), then play until the measure marked "**To Coda**," then skip to the section labelled "**Coda**."

D.S. al Fine — • Go back to the beginning of the song and play until the measure marked "**Fine**" (end).

Rhy. Fig. — • Label used to recall a recurring accompaniment pattern (usually chordal).

Riff — • Label used to recall composed, melodic lines (usually single notes) which recur.

Fill — • Label used to identify a brief melodic figure which is to be inserted into the arrangement.

Rhy. Fill — • A chordal version of a Fill.

tacet — • Instrument is silent (drops out).

• Repeat measures between signs.

1. | 2. — • When a repeated section has different endings, play the first ending only the first time and the second ending only the second time.

NOTE: Tablature numbers in parentheses mean:
1. The note is being sustained over a system (note in standard notation is tied), or
2. The note is sustained, but a new articulation (such as a hammer-on, pull-off, slide or vibrato begins, or
3. The note is a barely audible "ghost" note (note in standard notation is also in parentheses).